OUR GOVERNMENT

President

Fountaindale Public Library
Bolingbrook, IL
(630) 759-2102

by Kirsten Chang

BLASTOFF! READERS

BELLWETHER MEDIA • MINNEAPOLIS, MN

Blastoff! Readers are carefully developed by literacy experts to build reading stamina and move students toward fluency by combining standards-based content with developmentally appropriate text.

Level 1 provides the most support through repetition of high-frequency words, light text, predictable sentence patterns, and strong visual support.

Level 2 offers early readers a bit more challenge through varied sentences, increased text load, and text-supportive special features.

Level 3 advances early-fluent readers toward fluency through increased text load, less reliance on photos, advancing concepts, longer sentences, and more complex special features.

★ **Blastoff! Universe**

Reading Level

Grade **K**

Grades **1–3**

Grade **4**

This edition first published in 2021 by Bellwether Media, Inc.

No part of this publication may be reproduced in whole or in part without written permission of the publisher. For information regarding permission, write to Bellwether Media, Inc., Attention: Permissions Department, 6012 Blue Circle Drive, Minnetonka, MN 55343.

Library of Congress Cataloging-in-Publication Data

Names: Chang, Kirsten, 1991- author.
Title: President / by Kirsten Chang.
Description: Minneapolis, MN : Bellwether Media, 2021. | Series: Blastoff! readers. Our government | Includes bibliographical references and index. | Audience: Ages 5-8 | Audience: Grades K-1 | Summary: "Developed by literacy experts for students in kindergarten through grade three, this book introduces the president to young readers through leveled text and related photos"–Provided by publisher.
Identifiers: LCCN 2019059319 (print) | LCCN 2019059320 (ebook) | ISBN 9781644872031 (library binding) | ISBN 9781681038278 (paperback) | ISBN 9781618919618 (ebook)
Subjects: LCSH: Presidents–United States–Juvenile literature.
Classification: LCC JK517 .C53 2021 (print) | LCC JK517 (ebook) | DDC 352.230973–dc23
LC record available at https://lccn.loc.gov/2019059319
LC ebook record available at https://lccn.loc.gov/2019059320

Editor: Rebecca Sabelko   Designer: Laura Sowers

Printed in the United States of America, North Mankato, MN.

Table of Contents

Who Is the President?   4

Duties   10

An Important Job   18

Glossary   22

To Learn More   23

Index   24

Who Is the President?

The president is the leader of the United States.

President
Donald Trump

5

They are head of the **executive branch**.

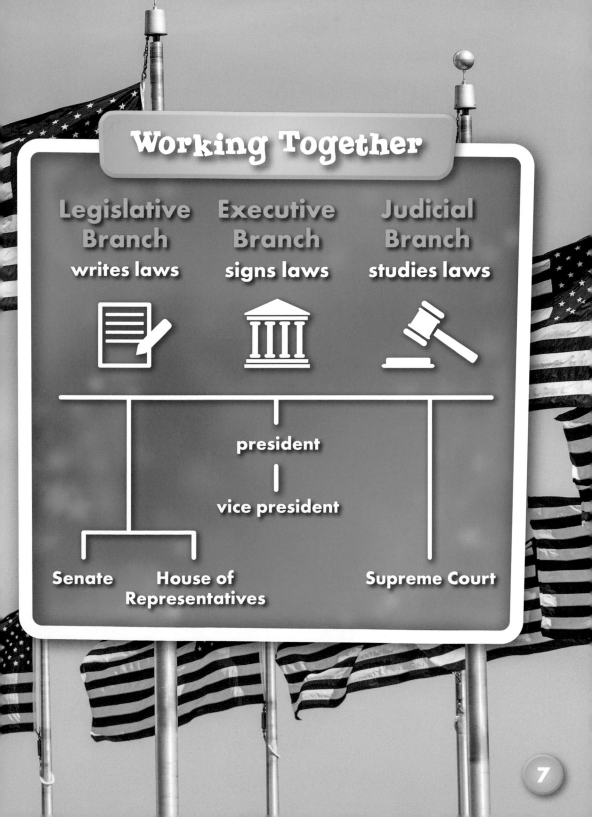

Working Together

Legislative Branch
writes laws

Executive Branch
signs laws

Judicial Branch
studies laws

president

vice president

Senate

House of Representatives

Supreme Court

7

Voters choose
the president
every four years.
The president can
serve two **terms**.

Must Haves

✓ **35 or older**

✓ **born in U.S.**

✓ **citizen at least 14 years**

**President
Ronald Reagan**

Duties

The president works in the White House. It is in Washington, D.C.

President
John F. Kennedy

11

The president meets
with leaders
of other countries.

President
Barack Obama

The **legislature** writes **laws**. The president signs them.

They lead the army.
They also suggest
judges for the
Supreme Court.

Supreme Court justice
Sonia Sotomayor

An Important Job

The president makes big **decisions**. Laws they pass are important.

President
Bill Clinton

The president works
for the people!

If I Were President ...

How would I lead?

Glossary

decisions

choices that someone makes

legislature

the part of government that writes laws

executive branch

the part of government that makes sure laws are followed

Supreme Court

the highest court in the United States where judges make sure laws are used fairly

laws

rules that people must follow

terms

fixed periods of time

To Learn More

AT THE LIBRARY
Bonwill, Ann. *We Have a Government.* New York, N.Y.: Children's Press, 2019.

Murray, Julie. *President.* Minneapolis, Minn.: Abdo Kids, 2018.

Schuh, Mari. *The White House.* Minneapolis, Minn.: Bellwether Media, 2019.

ON THE WEB

FACTSURFER

Factsurfer.com gives you a safe, fun way to find more information.

1. Go to www.factsurfer.com.

2. Enter "president" into the search box and click 🔍.

3. Select your book cover to see a list of related content.

Index

army, 16

countries, 12

decisions, 18

executive branch, 6

If I Were, 21

judges, 16

laws, 14, 18

leader, 4, 12

legislature, 14

Must Haves, 9

Supreme Court, 16

terms, 8

United States, 4

voters, 8

Washington, D.C., 10

White House, 10

Working Together, 7

works, 10, 20

years, 8

The images in this book are reproduced through the courtesy of: Orhan Cam, front cover; Evan El-Amin, pp. 4-5; Andriy Blokhin, pp. 6-7; American Photo Archive/ Alamy, pp. 8-9; Stocktrek Images, Inc/ Alamy, pp. 10-11; dpa picture alliance/ Alamy, pp. 12-13; MediaPunch Inc/ Alamy, pp. 14-15; American Photo Archive/ Alamy, pp. 16-17; ZUMA Press, Inc./ Alamy, pp. 18-19; White House Photo/ Alamy, pp. 20-21; fizkes, p. 22 (decisions); Joe Shom, p. 22 (executive branch); Freedomz, p. 22 (laws); NotarYES, p. 22 (legislature); artboySHF, p. 22 (Supreme Court); mizar_21984, p. 22 (term).